Embroidered Houses

Embroidered Houses

BETTY WOOLCOCK

SALLY MILNER PUBLISHING

First published in 2002 by
Sally Milner Publishing Pty Ltd
PO Box 2104
Bowral NSW 2576
AUSTRALIA

© Betty Woolcock 2002

Design and illustrations by Anna Warren, Warren Ventures
Edited by Anne Savage
Photography by Sergio Santos

Printed in China

National Library of Australia Cataloguing-in-Publication data:
Woolcock, Betty.
    Embroidered houses.

    ISBN 1 86351 301 9.

    1. Embroidery - Patterns. 2. Buildings in art. 3. Gardens
    in art. 4. Dwellings - Queensland. 5. Public buildings -
    Queensland. 6. Gardens - Queensland. I. Title. (Series :
    Milner craft series).

    746.44041

10 9 8 7 6 5 4 3 2 1

Contents

Foreword

*I*n recent years there has been a huge growth in the number of people involved in creative crafts of all kinds. Clubs for men and women catering for everything from woodworking to quilting are attracting large memberships. At the various craft markets around the country the creative skills of hundreds of people are displayed.

In every field there are those whose creativity and ability are exceptional. Betty Woolcock is such a one—a particularly gifted person in floral art, appliqué, quilting and embroidery. Her work has been acclaimed both here and overseas. She has shown a genius for design and colour and her work is exquisite in detail and execution.

Betty has two lovely personal qualities. One is her calm and gentle disposition even in the most stressful circumstances. The other is her great generosity in sharing freely with others her knowledge and skills and helping them explore and develop their own creative talents.

This book details but one aspect of her considerable ability and will bring pleasure not only to those who share her passion for this work but to anyone with a love of beautiful craftsmanship.

DONALD N. SHEARMAN OBE

Acknowledgments

I dedicate this book to my dear mother, Emilee Moller, who encouraged me to observe and love nature and all things beautiful, including the trees and the flowers, and to my father, who taught me perspective drawing.

I am indebted to my family and the many friends who have encouraged me, and especially to my husband Bryan for his patience in picking up many dropped threads and his invaluable assistance in collating this production.

This book would not have been published without the inspiration provided by Robyn Ginn and Diane Lampe, the encouragement of Danielle Chiel, and my many friends who enjoy sharing their craft skills with me and with each other.

My thanks go to Jonathon Larsen, whose pen sketches of old Queensland homes inspired me to embroider old houses after I had completed my six homes, which became part of the wall hanging reproduced in this book.

Introduction

My introduction to embroidery was not encouraging—my Grade 2 teacher held up my first effort to the class as a lesson on what not to do. Although this was a humiliating experience, she later encouraged me to persevere. My mother was a talented artist who taught me to paint and to appreciate colour and beauty. My own artistic talent was realised in floral art—as the proprietor of several businesses as a florist and as a teacher of floral art. In retirement I sought new forms of expression; finding quilting and a renewed interest in embroidery, I managed successfully to combine both. My sketching skills enabled me to enjoy drawing houses, including the six in which I have lived and many charming old Queenslanders. These lent themselves beautifully to being depicted in embroidery—with a degree of artistic licence allowing the simultaneous flowering of all the shrubs and trees in their gardens. My mother encouraged me to paint with brushes but I prefer to paint with my needle and thread and I love to pass on any skills I have.

Getting Started

I would love to encourage readers to embroider their own homes and gardens or even their front entrance as a first step. It is such a thrill and not too difficult. My embroidered homes range from early pioneer houses to old Queenslanders and my own modern home.

I suggest following the steps outlined here to help you achieve a satisfying result:

1. Take at least two photographs of the house you wish to embroider.

2. Have the photograph whose composition you prefer enlarged to the required size by photocopying.

3. Make a list of all the trees, shrubs and flowering plants in the garden. Artistic licence will allow you to have all of them flowering at the same time.

4. Cut a piece of ecology cloth or fine linen to the size required.

5. Use one of the following methods to transfer the photograph on to the fabric:

   (a) Use a ruler, set square and finely sharpened 2B pencil (I use an 0.5 mm Pentel PG 305) to measure and copy the photo.

   (b) Tape the photograph to a clear glass window, centre and tape the corners of the fabric over the photo and trace the house onto it with ruler and 2B pencil.

   (c) Tape the photograph to a clear glass table top with a lamp positioned beneath it, centre and tape the corners of the fabric over the photo and trace the house onto it with ruler and 2B pencil. At a pinch you could do this with a sheet of clear glass on your lap replacing the table.

   (d) It would be worth investing in a light box if you intend to do any number of embroideries of this type.

6. Shadows are copied using a 6B pencil, starting lightly and slowly darkening them. I work the roof line, guttering, railings and any trim in their original colours, using a single thread of embroidery cotton.

7. The outline is worked in stem stitch, with guttering and veranda rails in two rows of stem stitch and railings in single-thread stem stitch in dark grey. All other features of the house are worked in dark and light grey, as all the colour required is supplied by the colourful garden flowers.

Tips for embroiderers

A good place to do your stitching is at night in front of television. It certainly stops me from nodding off! You must, however, work under a good craft light. If you have not got such a light, drop the hint to the family that it would make a welcome gift.

I suggest you choose needles as follows:

No. 9 embroidery crewel for general embroidery

No. 9 or 10 crewel for one-strand embroidery

No. 8 straw needles are preferred for bullion stitch.

I recommend the use of a 15 cm (6 inch) embroidery hoop to keep the fabric taut, especially when working French knots and colonial knots. Always remove the hoop when you have finished working an area or when ceasing work for any length of time, as a hoop left in position for any length of time will leave a mark on the fabric. You should always remove your needle from the fabric for the same reason.

I stress the importance of not running threads across the back of your fabric, for example, do not run thread from one stem to another. As the back of the work is not seen or judged, I start with a minute knot and finish with a slip stitch under the stitches at the back.

Although I have suggested using particular colours for the flowers and trees in Appendices 2 and 3, you should not feel compelled to stick to those colours. You may prefer to match your threads to slightly different coloured flowers in your garden, or to bring the colours of other leaves and flowers into your thread box for a different effect.

Everyone asks, 'How long did it take you?' My reply is always, 'What does it matter? The end result is so rewarding.'

Good embroidering all.

Bullion stitch

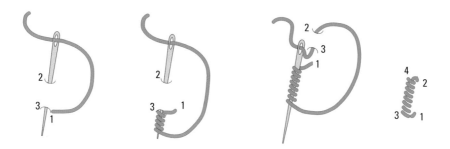

Make a back stitch the required length for the bullion stitch. Do not pull the needle right through the fabric.

Twist the thread the required number of twists in a clockwise direction, but not too tightly. Place your thumb over the wraps and pull the needle through firmly. Still holding the twisted thread, turn the needle back to the point of insertion (4) and insert in the same place to complete the stitch.

Buttonhole stitch

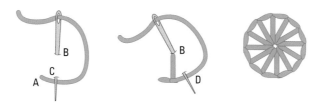

Bring the thread up from A, pull through and make a loop down and around to the right. Insert the needle at B, bring up to C with loop beneath the needle and pull through. Make a loop down and around to the right, insert needle again at B at the centre of the stitch, bring up at D and pull through. Continue until circle is complete and finish thread at the back.

Chain stitch

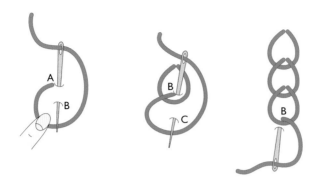

Bring the needle through at the starting point, hold the thread below and insert needle to one side close to starting point, bring up the needle over the thread to the required size of a loop of the chain, and repeat with even loops along the line of the chain.

Colonial knot

Easily achieved when using a 10 cm (4 inch) hoop. Bring the thread from the underside, hold thread with fingers of left hand and wrap two or more times around point of needle. Holding thread firmly, push the needle through the fabric and pull the thread through.

Couching

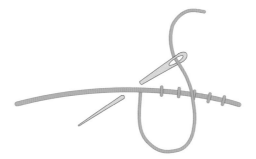

A small stitch used to hold another stitch in place, using the same colour thread.

Feather stitch

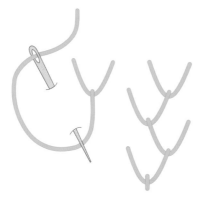

Bring the needle out at the top centre, hold the thread down with the left thumb, insert the needle a little to the right on the same level. Take a small stitch down to the centre, keeping the thread under the needle point. Next, insert the needle a little to the left on the same level and take a stitch to the centre, again keeping the thread under the needle point. Work these two movements alternately.

Fly stitch

Bring the thread through at the top left, hold it down with the left thumb, insert the needle to the right on the same level, a little distance from where the first thread emerged. Take a small stitch downwards to the centre with the thread below the needle. Pull through and insert the needle again below the stitch at the centre and bring it through in position for the next stitch. This stitch may be worked singly, in horizontal rows or vertically.

French knot

Bring the thread out at the required position, hold the thread down with your thumb and wrap it twice or more as in first diagram. Holding thread firmly, turn the needle back to the starting point and insert it close to where the thread first emerged. Pull thread through to the back and secure for a single knot or pass on to the next position.

Lazy daisy stitch

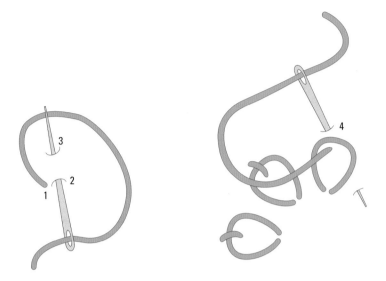

Bring your needle through where you want to start, work in the same manner as chain stitch (see chain stitch above) but work loops round in a circle. Fasten each loop at the base with a small stitch in the same colour.

Satin stitch

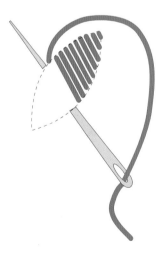

Satin stitch comprises a series of straight stitches worked closely together across the shape of the object being embroidered.

Scallop

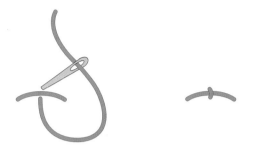

This is a straight stitch pulled into a curve by one or more couching stitches in the same thread colour.

Stem stitch

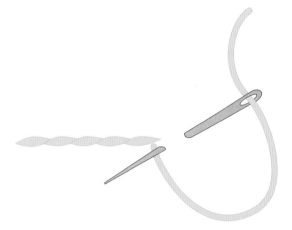

Stem stitch is worked from the left to the right of the pattern by making small even stitches.

1. 'My Life' Wall Hanging

My six homes became the subject of a much admired embroidered wall hanging, in the border of which I incorporated features which influenced my life while living in each house. These included my original two-teacher school, my high school in Maryborough, the Shakespeare Hotel at Barcaldine, where we lived for a time when first married, the Glennie School Kindergarten in Toowoomba where I was director, and St Paul's Cathedral, which occupied so much of my time in Rockhampton. My six homes and their associated features are included among the embroideries presented in this book. Also featured on the border are a representation of an appliquéd quilt to illustrate my dedication to this craft, a Tiger Moth aircraft to represent my flying days, and a florist's shopfront because of my long involvement in the flower industry.

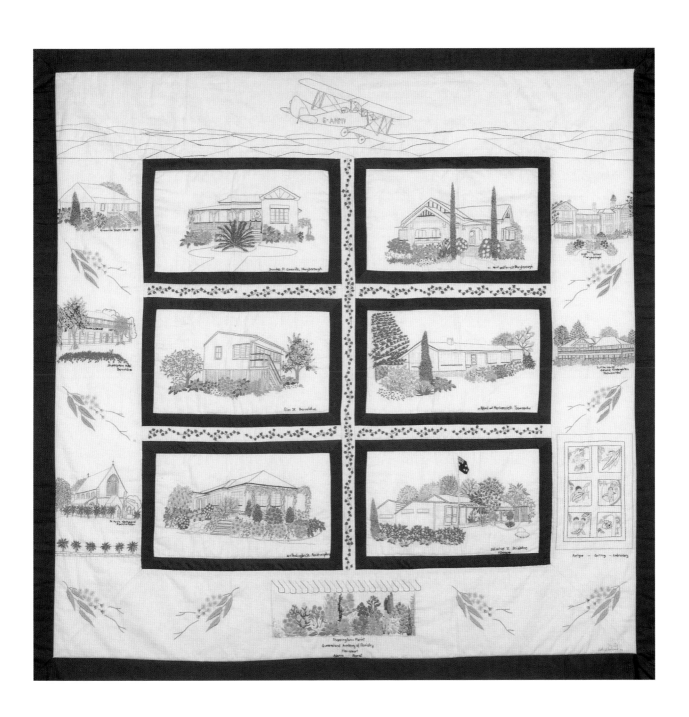

2. Dundas Street, Granville

My father designed and built our first home in 1925 in Granville, a suburb of Maryborough, about 200 kilometres north of Brisbane. It was a typical Queenslander of that period, with open verandas on two sides, a wooden frame, weatherboard walls and corrugated iron roof. I was actually born in the front room and have a sentimental attachment to my original home. My mother was the gardener and developed a much admired garden which was the setting for an annual garden party in aid of the local church. Included in the garden were wisteria, plumbago, hydrangea, hollyhocks, geraniums and roses. I show these in flower all at the same time, framing the magnificent palm that dominated the front garden.

Dundas St. Granville, Maryborough.

3. Granville State School, Maryborough

My parents were encouraged to enrol me in the local school at the age of four to boost the student numbers in order to retain the second teacher. The school was typical of the many small one- or two-teacher schools scattered throughout rural Queensland at that time. They were mostly built to a uniform design, a simple timber construction on timber stumps with a short flight of steps leading up to a small front veranda. In those days the building was surrounded by a carefully tended garden of hydrangeas, poinsettia, daisies, roses, numerous jacarandas and a pine tree.

Granville State School 1933

4. Kent and Ferry Streets, Maryborough

My building contractor father designed and built this more modern home in 1935, in a style typical of the period featuring stucco-finished brick construction and a terracotta tiled roof. located on a busy corner at the intersection of two major thoroughfares, the house was well known and the garden, once again designed and tended by my mother, much admired. It featured hydrangeas, daisies, petunias, daisies with a navy centre, roses, hibiscus, blue forget-me-nots, strelitzias, gardenias, gerberas, rondeletias, a wattle and two magnificent pencil pines framing the front entrance.

cr. Kent and Ferry St. Maryborough.

5. Maryborough Girls' High School

This school, the former Maryborough Girls' Grammar School, was conveniently situated directly opposite our home. The main building, shown here, was built in 1883 and remains as it was when I was a pupil there during the Second World War. I had been granted a trainee art teacher's scholarship and taught art while doing my senior studies. I decided that teaching was not what I really wanted to do, although the experience was to prove useful later. The magnificent Norfolk Island pines dominate the scene. The rose garden opposite the main entrance actually forms a full circle and the rest of the garden is always beautiful, with blue plumbago, hydrangeas and shasta daises completing the picture.

Girls
High School
Maryborough

6. The Shakespeare Hotel, Barcaldine

In 1952 I married Bryan, a veterinary surgeon, who was posted to Barcaldine in Central Western Queensland. The wool boom was on and housing almost impossible to obtain. I had been warned about the heat, the dust and the flies—but nobody mentioned the wonderfully hospitable people of the west. We lived at the Shakespeare, then the focus of many social activities, for some months waiting for a house to become vacant. The hotel is a landmark opposite the railway station. Outside it stands the famous gum tree, the 'Tree of Knowledge', under which the Australian Labor Party is said to have been formed during the great shearers' strike of 1891. The leaves of this tree can be seen on the left of the embroidery, which also includes a peltophorum (yellow poinciana) and a swathe of bright red bougainvillea.

Shakespeare Hotel
Barcaldine

7. Elm Street, Barcaldine

This quaint cottage on two-and-a-half metre stumps became the first home of our married life. It was affectionately known as the 'dove loft' and it served us well to entertain our many friends from the district. Luckily I was able to call on friends among the staff of the hospital across the road, or the local police sergeant's daughter, to keep me company during my husband's frequent work absences. Starting from scratch we developed an attractive garden with frangipani, hydrangea, daisies, gazanias and a variety of ferns. A yellow-flowered peltophorum on the footpath was a dominant feature. My husband started a thriving vegetable patch of tomatoes and cabbages— thriving when not being devoured by the town goats, that is! I was sorry to leave Barcaldine for the City of Toowoomba when Bryan was transferred.

Elm St. Barcaldine.

8. MacKenzie Street, Toowoomba

In Toowoomba we designed our own home (under the critical eye of my father) and planned a magnificent garden which developed quickly in the fertile red basaltic soil and benign climate of the 'garden city'. Our block of land was dominated by a huge Norfolk Island pine. We developed an orchard containing a variety of stone fruit and citrus trees. The large garden of flowering shrubs and plants flourished and included a magnolia and a flowering peach, a pencil pine, lilac, gardenias, roses, hydrangeas, daisies, geraniums, agapanthus, diosma and hollyhocks. To my disappointment, my husband accepted a transfer to Rockhampton just as the garden and the fruit trees were maturing and the flowering trees blooming for the first time!

cr Alford and Mackenzie St. Toowoomba

9. Sutton House, Glennie Memorial School, Toowoomba

I had been a trainee teacher and had done voluntary work at a child-minding centre, which led to my being invited to take up a temporary position as director of the Glennie Kindergarten—a temporary position that lasted four years. The kindergarten was located in Sutton House, a fine wooden structure built in 1930, with dormitories above and the kindergarten and preparatory school on the ground floor. During the Second World War it was taken over by the government and served as a military hospital. Before it was demolished in 1979, Sutton House was framed by silky oaks, Norfolk Island pines and jacarandas, and had a colourful garden of climbing roses, hydrangeas, gerberas and annuals of many kinds and colours.

'Sutton House'
Glennie Kindergarten
Toowoomba

10. The Range, Rockhampton

When we arrived in Rockhampton, we were lucky to find a home in an elevated
position facing east with a magnificently landscaped garden. Despite warnings about
Rockhampton's heat and humidity, we had a cool house where we spent seven
enjoyable years in this much maligned city. The garden featured a rare standard wisteria,
clerodendrum, jasmine, hydrangeas, white ixora, wattle, shasta daisies, poinsettia,
oleander, pigface and several bookleaf pines. A trellis covered with allamanda provided
a shaded walkway around two sides of the house. Once again we had to pack up, this
time to move to Brisbane.

61A Penlington St. Rockhampton

11. St Paul's Cathedral, Rockhampton

During our time in Rockhampton I became involved in charity work associated with St Paul's and the Rockhampton diocese and made many friends in the congregation, particularly among a wonderful group of women who ran a bargain store to raise funds. The original wooden church on the site, opened in 1862, was replaced with a church built of Stanwell freestone. The new building was consecrated in 1883 but did not become a cathedral until 1892 with the arrival of the first Bishop. The cathedral garden features pink cassia and jacarandas, with its many palms giving it a tropical appearance.

St. Pauls Cathedral
Rockhampton

12. My House, Kenmore

My sixth and present home is a modern bungalow in the Brisbane suburb of Kenmore, a little too large for our needs now that our two children are married with families of their own. It is very comfortable with a semi-enclosed veranda where I spend much time embroidering. I am particularly fond of the fernery and orchids at one end of the veranda. The garden is composed largely of shrubs that require little maintenance. The house is framed by lagerstroemia, wattle, pink and white frangipani, pink hibiscus and, until recently, a huge mango tree. The front is dominated by a large petrea, dracaena, strelitzia and two pink flowering gums, with poinsettias, gerberas, ixoras, mussaenda, blue boy and lavender. We fly our flag with great pride on special occasions.

23 Lochiel St. Brisbane
Kenmore

13. My Florist Shops

At various stages of my life I have been involved in floristry, both as an owner of businesses and as the founder and principal of the Queensland Academy of Floristry which I established in 1982. At various times I have attended courses at the Australian Academy of Floral Design, the Professional Floral Design School at Oklahoma City in the United States and the Constance Spry School in the United Kingdom. My involvement in this industry is represented by this shopfront with its awning sheltering masses of daisies, gerberas, proteas, agapanthus, arum lilies, rhododendron, clivia, red-hot pokers, sunflowers, hydrangea, strelitzia, arum lilies, delphinium, tulips, violets, pussy willow, snow drops, cornflowers and lavender.

Shoppingtown Florist
Queensland Academy of Floristry
Floramart
Adoria   Florist

14. Gumnut Babies

I retired from floral art and soon afterwards came under the influence of the talented Robyn Ginn, which completely changed the direction of my life. She taught me the craft of appliqué quilting, taking me back to needle and thread after many years. The gumnut babies quilt was one of my first efforts. I have since crafted many quilts, including several embroidered ones which have been much admired. I had found embroidery once again and was enjoying the experience immensely. Although my husband had retired from a busy professional life, he became active as a volunteer with his professional association, a professional educational college, a large charity and his lawn bowls club, so it was just as well I had my own interests. I was of course pleased when he was awarded the OAM for his services to his profession and to the community.

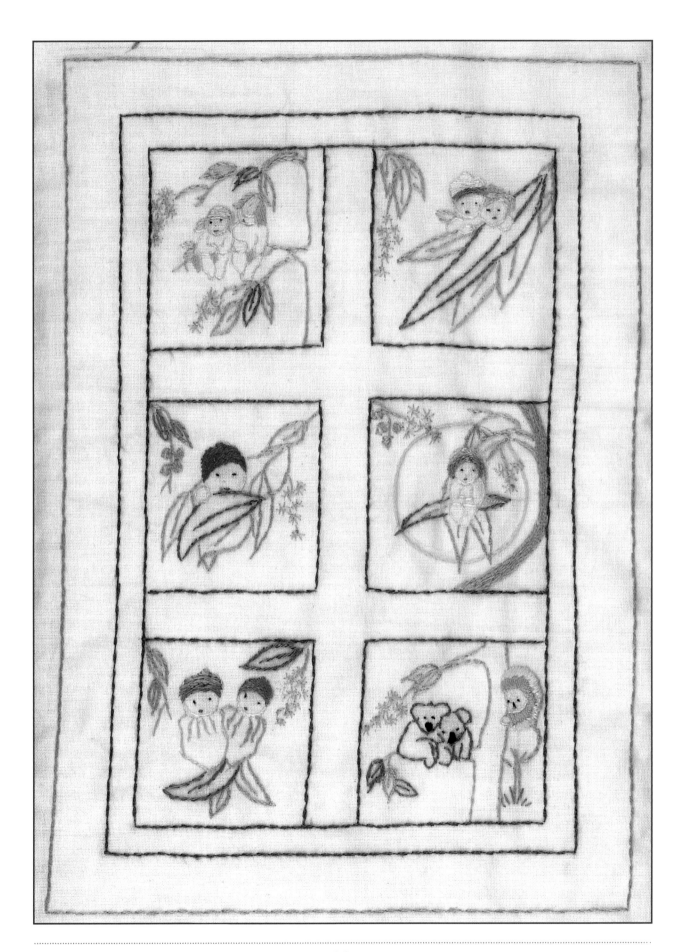

15. Pioneer Hut

The first homes built by the pioneers were of local timber shaped with an adze with a bark roof held down with timber. Some examples of these pioneer log huts still remain, some of them restored and others forming part of present-day homesteads. It was not unusual for natural knot holes in the timber to be left open so that rifles or shotguns could be fired through them for protection against bushrangers and others who might threaten isolated settlers. Many huts were primitive in the extreme, with only one earthen-floored room to provide shelter. Cooking and other domestic activities were conducted in a lean-to at the back of the hut, or in the open. The huts were eventually enlarged, and dividing walls added to provide privacy, but living remained basic. The native grass tree and the gum trees shown here would have been as close to a garden as most pioneers ever got.

Pioneers Hut

16. O'Reilly's Log Hut

This is the original bark-roofed hut built by the O'Reilly family in 1911 when they took up land for dairying on Roberts Plateau amid the subtropical rainforest of the McPherson Range near the Queensland—New South Wales border. The hut had a boot-scraper commonly placed at the entrance of country houses to keep out the mud and a hitching post for the horses. It is a more elaborate version of the simple pioneer log hut, built up off the ground and divided into three rooms. The hut is framed by straight-trunked trees of the dense subtropical forest of the area.

The O'Reilly family is famous for its part in the Stinson air crash rescue of 1937 and for the well-known O'Reilly's Resort, located adjacent to the Lamington National Park which was gazetted in 1915. Pat O'Reilly eventually built a more permanent wood slab dwelling near the site of the original hut. The descendants of the original settlers are still involved in the area, conducting the resort and the winery illustrated in embroidery 19.

17. The Mud Brick House

In areas of Queensland where suitable soils were present, a mud brick house provided a
more substantial home than the log hut. It often included a fireplace and stone
chimney and invariably an attached veranda with wooden veranda posts. Once again
the bark roof was secured with timber slabs. In this example the shaded windows
suggest that the house is probably divided into at least four rooms. The nearby windmill
to supply water is a normal part of the homestead scene. Typically, limited water
supplies and heavy work-loads did not encourage the establishment of gardens,
although in this case the settler's wife had attempted to grow native straw daisies and a
few shrubs. The gum trees already on the site provided shade.

18. Gracemere Homestead

A wonderful example of a pioneer home faithfully preserved by the descendents of the original settlers is provided by the Archer family's Gracemere homestead, a few kilometres west of Rockhampton. The home was designed by Colin Archer, the famous naval architect who designed the ship which was used by Amundsen for his Antarctic voyage. The homestead was built of adzed ironbark slabs, with interior walls of native plum cut on the property, and was first occupied by the Archer family in 1858. The garden has been described as a tranquil paradise sweeping down to the Gracemere lake on two sides. It features tree-shaded walks, masses of bougainvillea of various shades, a palm tree, jacaranda, wisteria, gum trees and native shrubs.

I am indebted to the late Edith Neish, whose wonderful pen sketches of the homes and buildings of Rockhampton and the surrounding district include one of the Gracemere homestead on which I have based this embroidery of the beautiful garden.

19. Killowen, Canungra Valley Vineyards

Killowen was built near Warwick in 1858 for the Devine family, who lived there for sixty-five years. The house is famous for its ghost, whose picture hangs in the hallway. This young woman is said to have stood next to the photographer when the picture was being taken. She died before the photo was developed and somehow her image appeared in the photo. The house was moved in three pieces from the Warwick district to its present location at O'Reilly's winery near Canungra in 1989 and has been faithfully restored, using many of the original features and antiques. The wide front veranda is now used as a restaurant, two rooms for private dining parties, the large ballroom for weddings, group wine tastings and functions, and the 'Cellar Door' for wine and gourmet food tastings. The new garden features gardenias along the entire front. The background of subtropical bushland, with a silky oak and jacarandas, provides a framework for the building.

20. The Worker's Cottage

This farmhouse, reminding me of my aunt's home on a farm near Eumundi, south of Gympie, is typical of many built across rural Queensland in the first half of the twentieth century. Constructed of milled timber on timber stumps, with a corrugated iron roof, they invariably had a small front veranda with a central passage leading to the kitchen-dining area, with two rooms on either side of the passage. The laundry was under the house and the earth closet was 'out the back'. As the farms prospered and new homes were built, the little original farmhouse became the farm employee or worker's cottage. The garden was often very sparse because the water supply was limited. In this case the garden includes an umbrella tree, palm tree, dracaenas, frangipani, hydrangea, wisteria, bananas, a jacaranda and a gum tree.

21. The Farmhouse, Bundaberg

Another frequently seen style of Queensland farmhouse is represented by this one near Bundaberg belonging to my uncle and aunt. Typical of these houses are the galvanised iron water-tank and the sheet-metal stove recess built onto the kitchen for fire safety and coolness. Dead eucalypts and other trees on the farm were felled and cut with a crosscut saw to provide fuel for the wood-burning stove. My aunt was famous for her beautiful garden on which she used every drop of recycled household water—saved because of the farm's limited water supply. She and her husband were cane and small crop farmers who endured the spartan life of those times with remarkable resolve and optimism. In the garden of this farmhouse can be seen wattle, frangipani, jacaranda, an umbrella tree, gum trees, Norfolk Island pines, a pencil pine, lemon tree, red roses, pink and blue hydrangeas, poinsettia, may bush, a very lovely old wisteria and an ipomoea climbing over the nearby shed.

22. Bethany, Kingaroy

This Queensland farmhouse is famous as the original home of the Honourable Sir Joh Bjelke-Petersen, a long-term Premier of Queensland. Built in 1913 and situated a few kilometres from the town of Kingaroy, noted for its peanuts, it attracts many busloads of visitors to view the home and property of Sir Joh and Lady Florence, herself notable as a Queensland Senator in the Federal Parliament. The house has undergone some changes in recent years and is now occupied by other members of the Bjelke-Petersen family. Sir Joh and Lady Flo have moved to another home nearby. The garden is well tended, featuring many rose bushes, allamanda and hydrangeas. The many surrounding trees include jacaranda, eucalypts, pencil pines, a bunya pine and a Norfolk Island pine.

23. Foundation Building, Gatton College

This landmark Federation style building was designed by the noted Scottish architect John Smith Murdoch. He later designed the provisional Parliament House in Canberra, which ended up being used by the Australian Parliament until 1988. Murdoch designed many other public buildings throughout Queensland, including the Maryborough Customs House and several provincial Court Houses. The Foundation Building, known until 1978 as the Administration Building, comprised two lecture rooms, library, study, principal's office and a visitor's room. The foundation stone was laid in 1896 and the building and the College opened in 1897. This building is significant as the oldest tertiary education building in Queensland and for its preservation in its original form. The College marked the government of the day's commitment to rural-based education. It is now a truly tertiary institution, being a campus of the University of Queensland. The two Canary Island palms flanking the Foundation Building were planted in 1915. The well-established and carefully tended gardens feature wattle, poinsettia, hydrangeas, roses, daisies, frangipani and jacaranda.

24. The Classic Queenslander

A plentiful supply of suitable building timbers and sensible adaptation to the climate led to the development in Queensland of a unique style of wooden home built above the ground on wooden posts and characterised by wide verandas on two or more sides. They were often ornately finished with cast iron, much of which arrived from Britain as ship's ballast. Warrawee, in the Brisbane suburb of Toowong, is a beautifully preserved example of ornate nineteenth-century design, demonstrating the wide verandas, intricate cast iron baluster panels and ornate veranda-post capitals (or heads) typical of the classical Queenslander. The garden features a leopard tree and gardenia bushes on either side of the front steps.

25. Mien Street, Spring Hill

This well-preserved example of an early Brisbane city residence is located in the inner suburb of Spring Hill. Of wooden construction with a corrugated iron roof, and standing on timber stumps, it displays many of the characteristics of nineteenth-century architecture. The front veranda with its bull-nosed iron roof, wooden balustrade and intricate patterned fretwork above the front gate is typical of the period. A more recent addition is the enclosure of the veranda by lattice to provide privacy and security. The lattice gate leads to a central corridor with rooms on either side that leads to the kitchen and dining room at the rear of the house. The laundry is under the house. It has been owned by the family of Dr Paul Spiro for some fifty years and has seen a succession of tenants. One side of the house is framed by a jacaranda, the other by a frangipani. The front veranda is adorned with a pink cluster climbing rose and a wisteria vine. Against the front fence are a hydrangea and ferns.

26. Leichhardt Street, Spring Hill

This residence in the inner suburb of Spring Hill was made famous as the home of the late Cecilia Elizabeth McNally, who purchased the property in 1965. For many years the heart and soul of Spring Hill, she was the initiator, organiser and driving force behind the famous Spring Hill Fair, held each year on the streets of this suburb which adjoins the Central Business District. The Fair was extremely popular with the residents of Brisbane and beyond and raised considerable sums of money for charities nominated by Miss McNally. The block of land, dating back to 1860 in the early history of the city, is now occupied by four modern city apartments bearing little resemblance to the old residence. This embroidery is based on Jonathon Larsen's pen sketch of the home in its former glory, when the garden featured roses, hydrangeas, daisies, lavender, frangipani, a peach tree, allamanda and a jacaranda.

27. Cricket Street Terraces, Milton

These terrace houses, built in the inner Brisbane suburb of Milton, are among the few examples of ornate terraces in the city and nearby suburbs which are obviously of English influence. They feature elaborate cast iron balustrades and tiled roofs of imported materials, some of which were brought out as ship's ballast. All were of two-storey brick construction, usually with bay windows and tiny decorative balconies or verandas often too small for outdoor living. Each terrace has a small front garden with hydrangeas, white roses, pink magnolia, ivy, hibiscus and wisteria, with two gum trees towering above.

28. Howard Street, Rosalie

The older inner suburbs of Brisbane are worth searching for gems of nineteenth-century architecture, some more ornate than others. This lovely residence at Rosalie enjoys a panoramic view of Milton, Paddington and the City of Brisbane beyond and is a well-maintained example of the more decorative style of Queenslander sometimes still to be found in the inner city. The elaborate rotundas at both front corners of the dwelling are striking in effect. I have taken some liberties with the garden to enhance the impact of the embroidery. The beautiful poinciana tree dominating the front garden is sadly no longer there. There is a climbing red rose along the side veranda, with hydrangeas, agapanthus, roses, daisies, a flowering peach tree, wisteria, lavender and forget-me-nots. Jonathon Larsen's pen sketch was the inspiration for this embroidery.

29. Euralia, Norman Park

Built about 1889, this heritage-listed classic Victorian mansion is located on a hilltop in Norman Park, an inner Brisbane suburb. It is a well-known landmark, having been used as a popular reception centre. Euralia is surrounded by some half a hectare of beautifully maintained gardens and century old trees. The verandas are richly decorated and provide summer shade, winter sun and adequate space for informal entertainment. The classic features include tessellated tiling, an ornately lead-lighted entry hall and the elaborate red cedar joinery frequently encountered in Queensland homes of this period. The garden features a wonderful standard wisteria, potted cumquat trees by the front porch, camellias, a pine tree, wattle, jacarandas, hydrangeas, roses, shasta daisies and many old established trees.

30. Wanora, Indooroopilly

This beautifully symmetrical design is typical of the very early twentieth century. It was built of the finest timbers with a wide veranda around three sides, and front steps of timber rising to a door leading to a central passage and rooms on either side. The balusters are wooden, as are the veranda post-heads and the arch over the front entrance, which is capped by a typical gable of that time. The house was sold for removal in 1987 and now commands a semi-rural scene in the Samford valley. This was an unfortunate outcome for the suburb, as the land was redeveloped with multiple brick units of a less than attractive appearance. The original garden was graced by a large weeping fig, which was removed to make way for the unit development. The house was framed by gum trees at the rear and a natural bush hedge along one side, and a lovely cassia tree. The front garden featured pink and blue hydrangeas, shasta daisies, forget-me-nots, poinsettia and roses.

31. Smithfield, Toowoomba

This heritage-listed home is one of Australia's finest examples of late nineteenth-century classic colonial architecture. Smithfield was designed as a private home by local architect James Marks for Darling Downs pastoralist, Toowoomba mayor and long-serving member of the Queensland Parliament, James Taylor. The 97-square building has bluestone foundations 4 metres (13 feet) deep, external bluestone walls with sandstone detailing to bays and corners, and high metal lath ceilings. Window frames, elegant doors and architraves are in red cedar, and the entrance hall features intricate black and white parquetry flooring. Smithfield has had a chequered history since it was built in 1890. It was at one time occupied by an Austrian nobleman and several families. During the Second World War and for several years after it housed the Anglican Glennie Preparatory School. It was operated as a well-known restaurant for many years but now has private owners who are painstakingly restoring the homestead as a private residence. The Smithfield gardens are always filled with beautiful flowers, among them agapanthus, magnolia, roses, violets, may bush, black-eyed Susan hydrangeas and daisies. The trees include jacaranda, cypress pine, gums and palms. The old German wagon has been a feature of the garden for many years.

32. Westbrook Homestead

As early as 1840 John Campbell, Queensland's first squatter, selected over 44 000 hectares (110 000 acres) of the gently undulating black soil of the Darling Downs stretching westward from Toowoomba. The third owners of the selection, partners McLean and Beit, in 1867 built the existing heritage-listed homestead which has been admired by many for its stone walls and slate roof, imported from Wales, and red cedar doors and fittings. McLean was the member for Eastern Darling Downs in the Queensland Legislative Assembly and was at one time Colonial Treasurer. He and his partner both died as the result of unfortunate events and McLean is buried in the small homestead graveyard. The holding was gradually reduced in size by government acquisition or sale as it passed through two more partnerships, including Shanahan and Jennings, the latter at one time being Premier of New South Wales. It was purchased in 1949 by the McPhie family and later occupied by the McGuigan and Gifford families. The present owners are intent on restoring the somewhat neglected homestead, and also plan to restore the garden to its former glory. Artistic licence has been used to present the garden as it might develop. It features a holly tree, a jacaranda and a magnificent bunya pine. Also shown are camellias, roses (including a magnificent yellow banksias rose), hydrangeas and shasta daisies, interspersed with mauve lantana and agapanthus.

Appendix 1

This section lists all the flowers and shrubs depicted in the embroidered houses and gardens in this book and the stitches and threads used for each one. While I have specified the exact colours I have used, it is much better for you to make your own decision on colour once you have compared leaf, stem or flower with the available threads. Note that one thread is used for all stitchery unless stated otherwise. Unless otherwise indicated, work the stems/trunks first, then the leaves and then the flowers. See page XX for tips and requirements.

Agapanthus

A very popular garden plant in Australia as it flowers in early summer and over Christmas. It is usually grown in clumps to show the blue flowers to best effect. See embroideries 8, 13, 31 and 32.

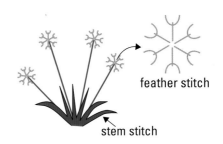

feather stitch

stem stitch

Threads .
DMC 341 *(mauve-blue)*
DMC 3348 *(mid green)*

I have worked the full heads of blue flowers in feather stitch in a circle and the long stems and leaves in double-row stem stitch.

Allamanda

A fast-growing evergreen scrambling climber with lance-shaped leaves of a mid-green shade, rich bright yellow flowers with five rounded petals and a trumpet throat in a darker shade of yellow. See embroideries 10, 22 and 26.

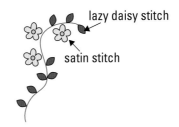

lazy daisy stitch

satin stitch

Threads

DMC 743 (yellow)

DMC 742 (dark yellow)

DMC 3347 (mid green)

The leaves are worked in satin stitch and the flowers embroidered in yellow lazy daisy stitch. The flower centre is worked with a three-wrap French knot in dark yellow.

Arum lily

This is a very old spring-flowering bulb. The flowers are an elongated white or cream trumpet shape, with a bright yellow spadix. See embroidery 13.

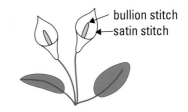

bullion stitch

satin stitch

Threads

White

DMC 745 (cream)

DMC 743 (bright yellow)

DMC 3374 (sap green)

The long leaves are sap green in colour and worked in satin stitch. The main part of the flower is worked in cream or white satin stitch. The central spadix is embroidered in bright yellow bullion stitch with 12 or 14 wraps, using two strands of thread.

Banksia rose

This is a climbing rose bearing clusters of rosettes of fully double yellow flowers. See embroidery 32.

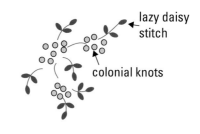

Threads

DMC 743 (bright yellow)
DMC 3347 (dark green)

The flowers are worked in three-wrap colonial knots in bunches of bright yellow. The leaves and stems are the same dark green in a lazy daisy stitch.

Black-eyed Susan

This is a fast-growing annual, a vigorous twining climber. It has oval to heart-shaped mid-green leaves and small rounded, rather flat, bright orange flowers with a dark centre. See embroidery 31.

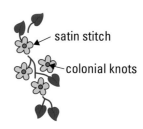

Threads

DMC 740 (orange)
DMC 3348 (mid green)
DMC 938 (dark brown)

I have worked the flower petals in orange satin stitch. The dark brown centres are done in three-wrap colonial knots; the mid-green leaves are worked in satin stitch.

Blue boy

This is a lovely, hardy perennial ground cover. See embroidery 12.

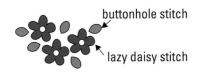

Threads

White
DMC 792 (dark blue)
DMC 3348 (mid green)

Work the leaves in mid-green lazy daisy stitch, and the flowers in dark blue buttonhole stitch with a centre in a three-wrap colonial knot in white.

Bougainvillea

This is a colourful and vigorous, evergreen, woody-stemmed scrambling climber. These days available in many colours, it is a magnificent sight in full bloom. The flower comprises three bracts of pure colour in oranges, pinks, reds, purples or white. The inner flower is tubular in shape with four petals. See embroideries 6 and 18.

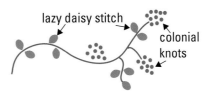

Threads

DMC 608 (orange)
DMC 961 (dark pink)
DMC 600 (red)
DMC 3348 (mid green)
DMC 610 (light brown)

The coloured bracts are worked in lazy daisy stitch in the required colour, and the tiny flowers are worked in white three-wrap colonial knots. The green leaves are done in lazy daisy in a soft mid green. The stems are worked in stem stitch in light brown.

Browallia

Commonly known as the bush violet, the rich blue flower of this shrub has a white eye and five flat petals in a rounded leaf shape. See embroidery 31.

eye: colonial knots

satin stitch

Threads

DMC 809 (rich blue)
White
DMC 3348 (mid green)

The petals are worked in rich blue satin stitch and the eye is a three-wrap colonial knot in white. Leaves are worked in mid-green satin stitch.

Camellia

A popular evergreen woody shrub or small tree with glossy deep green leaves and blooms of many colours. See embroidery 32.

two bullion stitches with 10 wraps

2 threads used for straight stitches around centre

Threads

White
DMC 962 (pink)
DMC 3347 (deep green)
DMC 611 (light brown)

The centre of the flower is worked with two bullion stitches in white or pink, using ten wraps (as for roses). The outer five petals are scallops worked with two threads around a central point with overlapping, small, slightly curved stitches. Stems are light brown stem stitch and the leaves are worked in satin stitch in deep green.

Camellia sasanqua

This type of camellia is a densely foliaged plant with small, shiny dark green leaves and small fragrant single flowers in a variety of colours. See embroidery 32.

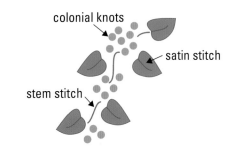

centre: 2 bullion stitches

satin stitch

outside petals:
straight stitch

Threads

DMC 605 (pink)

White

DMC 3362 (dark green)

DMC 611 (light brown)

The flowers are worked in pink or white similar to camellias, with two eight-wrap bullion stitches in the centre, and five scallops for the outer petals. Stems are light brown stem stitch. The leaves are worked in satin stitch in dark green.

Clerodendrum

The flowers of this prolific vine are borne in bright orange-red clusters. The sap-green leaves are carried on light brown stems. See embroidery 10.

colonial knots

satin stitch

stem stitch

Threads

DMC 608 (bright orange)

DMC 611 (light brown)

DMC 3364 (mid green)

The flowerheads are worked in colonial knots of two wraps in orange, the leaves in mid-green satin stitch and the vine stem in stem stitch of light brown.

Clivia

An evergreen with strap-shaped dark green leaves and flowers appearing in the centre of the leaf clump. The stems produce heads of 10 to 20 orange flowers in spring or early summer. They have six bright orange petals with pale orange centres. See embroidery 13.

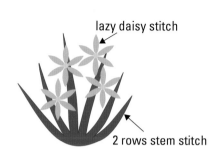

Threads

DMC 970 (bright orange)

DMC 972 (pale orange)

DMC 3362 (dark green)

The petals are worked in bright orange lazy daisy stitch, with single strokes of pale orange in each petal at the base of the flower. The leaves are worked in two rows of stem stitch in dark green.

Cornflower

Cornflower or centaurea, also known as knapweed, flowers in summer in colours of blue, mauve, crimson or white. See embroidery 13.

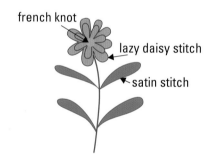

Threads

DMC 3053 (mid green)

DMC 3755 (mid blue)

DMC 842 (light brown)

The long leaves are worked in three strokes of satin stitch in mid green. The flowers are worked in two rows of lazy daisy stitch, the centre row being in smaller stitches. The centre is a French knot with three wraps in light brown.

Daisy

Three types of daisies appear in these embroideries—the shasta daisy, white with yellow centre; the blue-eyed daisy, white with blue centre; and the ground daisy, pink with yellow centre.

Threads

White
DMC 972 (bright yellow)
DMC 3364 (grey-green)
DMC 971 (navy blue)
DMC 3688 (pink)

The shasta daisy is worked in five white lazy daisy stitches with its centre a two-wrap yellow colonial knot, and long grey-green lazy daisy stitches for the leaves.

The blue-eyed daisy is worked in five white lazy daisy stitches with its centre a two-wrap navy blue colonial knot, and long grey-green lazy daisy stitches for the leaves.

The ground daisy is worked with buttonhole stitch petals in pink and a yellow centre of a two-wrap French knot.

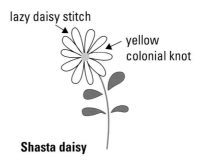

lazy daisy stitch

yellow colonial knot

Shasta daisy

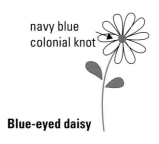

navy blue colonial knot

Blue-eyed daisy

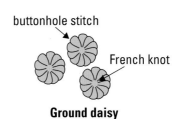

buttonhole stitch

French knot

Ground daisy

Delphinium

One of the most attractive of the cottage garden perennials, with tall showy spikes of flowers in varying shades of blue, pink or white. See embroidery 13.

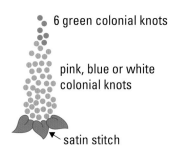

6 green colonial knots

pink, blue or white colonial knots

satin stitch

Threads

Any shade of pink, blue or white— suggest DMC 605 (pink) and DMC 341 (blue)

DMC 3348 (mid green)

Start from the top of the flower spike with mid green, working six colonial knots with three wraps. Change to pink, blue or white and continue working in colonial knots of three wraps for the full length of the flower spike. The leaves are mid-green satin stitch.

Diosma

A low-growing shrub grown for its dainty pink flowers and overall rounded appearance. See embroidery 8.

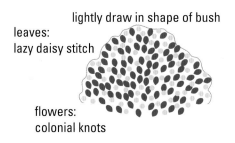

lightly draw in shape of bush

leaves: lazy daisy stitch

flowers: colonial knots

Threads

DMC 963 (light pink)

DMC 3348 (mid green)

The flowers are worked in two-wrap colonial knots in light pink, and mingled with very fine mid-green leaves in lazy daisy stitch. This shrub is so compact that no stems are visible.

Dracaena

A shrub or small tree with sword-like leaves forming a spiky head. It is great for potted house plants. See embroidery 12.

satin stitch

Threads

DMC 3024 (light grey-green)
DMC 3362 (mid green)

The heads of leaves are worked first in satin stitch and the limbs are worked around the trunk, from the bottom to the top, in light grey-green satin stitch.

Ferns

Sword fern is an evergreen fern with narrow, lance-shaped, divided herring-bone fronds. See embroideries 7 and 25.

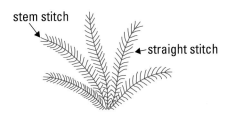

stem stitch

straight stitch

Threads

DMC 3348 (mid green)

The stems are worked in stem stitch first; then work the leaves in small straight stitches on either side of the stem, all in mid green.

Forget-me-not

Forget-me-not is a lovely little perennial border plant, forming compact masses of blue when in flower. See embroideries 4, 28 and 30.

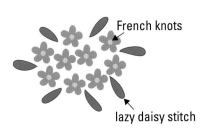

French knots

lazy daisy stitch

Threads

DMC 341 (blue)
DMC 3348 (mid green)
DMC 972 (bright yellow)

Forget-me-not has lance-shaped leaves worked in lazy daisy stitch in a mid-green shade. The heads of tiny five-petalled blue flowers are worked in two-wrap French knots with a bright yellow two-wrap French knot in the centre.

Gardenia

This popular slow-growing evergreen has beautiful glossy dark green leaves and very fragrant double white flowers. See embroideries 4, 8, 19 and 24.

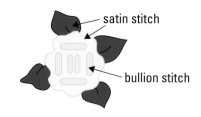

Threads

DMC 726 (soft cream)

DMC 3363 (dark green)

DMC 3828 (milk brown)

The centres of the all-cream flowers are worked in two bullions of ten wraps, surrounded by four bullion stitches each with twelve wraps, and the outside petals are worked in satin stitch. The leaves are worked in satin stitch. The stem is a milk-brown colour worked in stem stitch.

Gazania

This is a hardy border plant, a large daisy-like plant with flowers in bright colours of yellow, orange and pink. See embroidery 7.

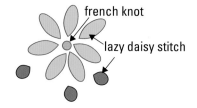

Threads

DMC 444 (bright yellow)

DMC 603 (deep pink)

DMC 972 (orange)

DMC 3348 (deep green)

The thin petals are worked in long bright yellow lazy daisy stitches. The leaves are done in a deep green lazy daisy stitch. The centre of the flower is a French knot of three wraps in orange.

Geranium

This plant, which flowers well in all climates, is grown throughout the world in pots, in window boxes and in the garden. It has multiple heads of flowers attached by fine green stalks to a central stem of dark green. See embroideries 2 and 8.

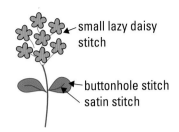

small lazy daisy stitch

buttonhole stitch
satin stitch

Threads

DMC 321 (bright red)
DMC 3733 (bright pink)
DMC 3348 (mid green)

The stalks are worked in one stroke of mid green under the flowerheads, and the stems in mid-green stem stitch. The flowers are worked in five petals in short, fat lazy daisy stitches in red or bright pink. The leaves are worked in mid-green buttonhole stitch.

Gerbera

This bright cheerful flower is an evergreen, erect perennial. Its flowers, with long daisy-like petals, come in many colours. See embroideries 4, 9, 12 and 13.

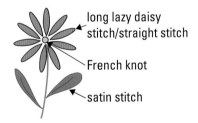

long lazy daisy stitch/straight stitch

French knot

satin stitch

Threads

DMC 962 (deep pink)
DMC 321 (bright red)
DMC 972 (deep yellow)
DMC 3348 (mid green)

The flowers are worked in long, thin lazy daisy stitch or straight strokes around a circular centre. The centre (depending on the size of the flower) is worked in French knots of one or more twists in deep yellow. The leaves are worked in mid-green satin stitch.

Hibiscus

There are many varieties and colours to choose from, both single and double, in this abundantly flowering plant. The shrub grows to nearly two metres with thick green foliage. The lovely medium to large flower has five petals in the single forms, many more in the double forms. See embroideries 4, 8, 12 and 27.

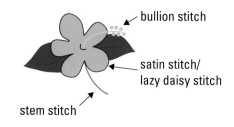

Threads

DMC 776 *(pink)*

DMC 899 *(dark pink)*

DMC 742 *(bright yellow)*

DMC 3346 *(dark green)*

DMC 524 *(grey-green)*

Smaller flowers are worked in pink or dark pink in lazy daisy stitch, larger flowers in satin stitch. From the centre place a yellow stamen in a straight stitch with a bullion stitch of five wraps at the 'free' end. The leaves are worked in dark green satin stitch. The stem is a grey-green stem stitch.

Hollyhock

This is a tall summer-flowering biennial with erect spikes of pink, crimson, yellow or white flowers and heart-shaped leaves. In spots sheltered from the wind it can grow as high as three metres. See embroideries 2 and 8.

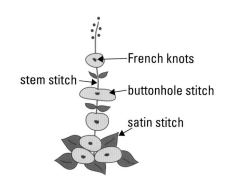

Threads

DMC 3316 *(pink)*

DMC 899 *(dark pink)*

DMC 472 *(soft green)*

The flower petals are worked in a pink buttonhole stitch with a darker pink French knot of one or two wraps in the centre. The leaves are worked in a soft green satin stitch. Stems are the same shade as the leaves in stem stitch.

Hyacinth

This is a bulbous plant of the lily
family native to Greece. My children liked
to grow them with the bulbs sitting on top
of a milk bottle filled with water. They
flowered beautifully. The hyacinth is a
handsome ornamental flower with a stout
stem bearing a dense, sweetly fragrant
cluster of pink, white or strong blue flowers
shaped like small flaring bells. See embroidery 13.

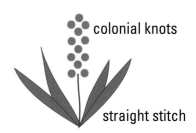

Threads

DMC 341 *(blue-purple)*
DMC 3716 *(pink)*
DMC 3363 *(mid green)*

The flowers are worked in colonial knots of two twists in the chosen colour of blue-
purple or pink. A large bulb sends up long narrow leaves, worked in mid-green
straight stitch in two threads, commencing at ground level.

Hydrangea

This hardy but shade-loving bushy
shrub, much used in Queensland
gardens, is available in many varieties.
It produces dense rounded heads of
pale blue, pink or white flowers. See
embroideries 2, 3, 4, 5, 7, 9, 10, 13, 20,
21, 22, 23, 25, 27, 28, 30, 31 and 32.

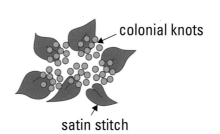

Threads

DMC 340 *(blue-mauve)*
DMC 962 *(bright pink)*
White
DMC 3364 *(bright green)*

The flowers are worked in groups of 7 to 10 colonial knots of three wraps in blue-
mauve or bright pink. The foliage is worked in bright green satin stitch. The bush is
so dense that you cannot see the stems.

Ipomoea

Also known as morning glory, this is a twining climber with bright green heart-shaped leaves and wide, circular, red, purple, pink or blue flowers. See embroidery 21.

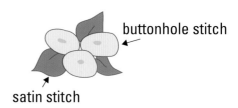

Threads

DMC 321 (red)
DMC 552 (purple)
DMC 963 (pale pink)
DMC 3746 (blue-purple)
DMC 726 (soft yellow)
DMC 989 (bright green)

The leaves are worked in bright green satin stitch, the flowers in buttonhole stitch in the colour of your choice with a yellow dot centre worked as a French knot with three twists.

Ivy

Ivy is a dense evergreen vine native to Europe and Asia. Many forms of the common ivy are grown as house plants. They are very hardy plants and adapt well anywhere. See embroidery 27.

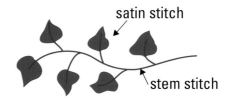

Threads

DMC 3362 (dark green)

Ivy has a three-lobed leaf and is worked in satin stitch in dark green. The stems are worked in stem stitch in the same colour.

Ixora

This evergreen rounded shrub has glossy dark green leaves up to 10 cm (4 inches) long. The small, tubular flowers in colours of red, pink, orange or yellow are produced in dense heads. See embroidery 10.

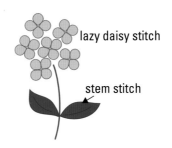

lazy daisy stitch

stem stitch

Threads

DMC 608 (deep orange)
DMC 326 (red)
DMC 3805 (deep pink)
DMC 725 (yellow)
DMC 3362 (dark green)

The leaves are worked in dark green stem stitch and the flowerheads in four small lazy daisy stitches in the colour of your choice.

Jasmine

This woody-stemmed scrambling climber is grown for its delicate and fragrant cream spring flowers and mid-green foliage. See embroidery 10.

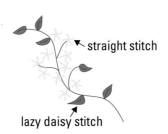

straight stitch

lazy daisy stitch

Threads

DMC 745 (cream)
DMC 3347 (mid green)

The flowers are worked in straight strokes in cream and the leaves in mid-green lazy daisy stitch.

Lantana

This is an evergreen rounded to spreading shrub with finely wrinkled deep green leaves. It has bunches of tiny tubular flowers, sometimes mauve or white, often red or orange. The small variety is not a robust grower like the common lantana that invades bushland, but is ideal as a ground cover. See embroidery 32.

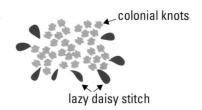

colonial knots

lazy daisy stitch

Threads

DMC 208 (lavender)

DMC 3362 (deep green)

The leaves are worked in deep green lazy daisy stitch; the flowers are best worked in two-wrap colonial knots in groups of seven.

Lavender

These lovely perennial shrubs are native to the Mediterranean region. They are grown both as ornamentals and commercially for their fragrant oils. They grow to about one metre high and have narrow greyish leaves. See embroideries 12, 13 and 28.

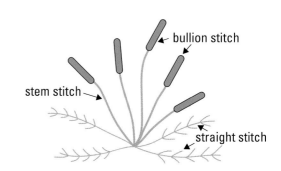

bullion stitch

stem stitch

straight stitch

Threads

DMC 208 (lavender)

DMC 209 (lilac)

DMC 3022 (silver-grey)

The leaves are worked in straight stitch in silver-grey. Stems are in stem stitch in the same shade. The numerous spikes of flowers are worked in bullion stitch with ten wraps in lavender or lilac.

Lilac

Lilac is a bushy deciduous shrub with long bunchy heads of beautiful fragrant four-petalled flowers in pink, white or lilac. The leaves are heart-shaped, in a mid-greyish green shade. See embroidery 8.

Threads
White
DMC 3689 (pink)
DMC 209 (lilac)
DMC 3013 (grey-green)
DMC 738 (bone)

The flowers have four petals but because of their small size are worked in pink or lilac colonial knots. The leaves are worked in grey-green lazy daisy stitch. The stems are bone in colour and worked in stem stitch.

May bush

This attractive shrub (Spiraea) looks like a mound of snow when in full flower. It produces small bunches of double white flowers on long, arching canes. See embroideries 21 and 31.

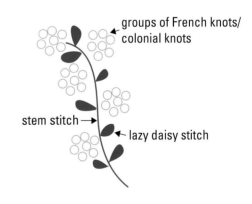

Threads
White
DMC 3362 (dark green)
DMC 642 (light brown)

You can work the white flowers with either five one-wrap colonial knots or five French knots. The tiny leaves are a dark green and are worked in lazy daisy stitch. The stems are in one-thread straight stitch in light brown.

Murraya

This popular plant can be grown as a hedge or as a bush. The small bunches of highly perfumed white flowers, similar to orange blossoms, often seem to appear when rain threatens.

Threads
White
DMC 3362 (dark green)
DMC 3072 (green-grey)

The flowers are worked in five petals of lazy daisy stitch. The leaves are worked in dark green satin stitch on stems of green-grey stem stitch, five to a stem.

Mussaenda

A lovely shrub of varying coloured leaves and bracts. See embroidery 12.

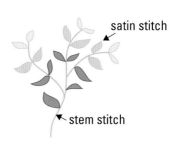

Threads
DMC 3045 (cream-brown)
DMC 951 (cream-pink)
DMC 225 (soft pink)
DMC 3347 (mid green)

All leaves and bracts are worked in satin stitch. The top new bracts are in cream-pink, the next are soft pink and the leaves in mid green. The stems are done in cream-brown stem stitch.

Oleander

This evergreen shrub, once common in older gardens but seen less often these days because of its toxicity, has long, thin, deep green leaves and clusters of flowers in pink, white, red or apricot. See embroidery 10.

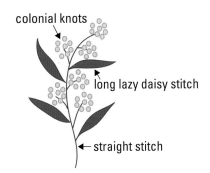

Threads
White
DMC 321 (red)
DMC 352 (apricot)
DMC 3362 (dark green)
DMC 370 (mid brown)

The leaves are worked in dark green in a long lazy daisy stitch, the five-petalled flowers in groups of colonial knots in the chosen colour. The stem is worked in mid-brown straight stitch.

Osteospermum

This is an evergreen upright perennial similar to gazania. The daisy-like flowers have white or yellow petals, and a dark blue centre around a yellow central 'eye'. See embroidery 7.

petals and leaves: lazy daisy stitch
centre: French knot surrounded
by circle of small stem stitches

Threads
White
DMC 742 (bright yellow)
DMC 792 (dark blue)
DMC 3364 (mid green)

The flower has ten to twelve petals which are worked in lazy daisy stitch in bright yellow or white. Work the centre of the flower with a bright yellow French knot with three wraps. A one-thread dark blue circle is worked around the centre with small stem stitches. The mid-green foliage is worked in lazy daisy stitch.

Petrea

This is a lovely climber with rich deep bluish purple flowers in long bunches. The individual flower has five flat petals and when mature spirals to the ground like a helicopter rotor. In the centre is a smaller rounded deep purple petal with a central white spot. See embroidery 12.

Threads

White

DMC 341 (blue-lavender)

DMC 792 (blue-purple)

DMC 580 (mid green)

DMC 372 (creamy brownish green)

satin stitch

2-thread straight stitch
colonial knot with French knot centre

The flowers are worked in elongated bunches. The outer petals are worked in two threads, in five straight stitches in blue-lavender. Place a three-wrap colonial knot of blue-purple in the middle and finish with a white one-wrap French knot at the centre point. The vine is worked in two threads of creamy brownish green in stem stitch and the leaves are done in mid-green satin stitch.

Petunia

A quick-growing annual with trumpet-shaped flowers in a variety of colours in spring. See embroidery 4.

Threads

White

DMC 3779 (pink)

DMC 3364 (green)

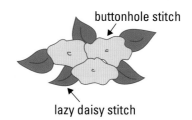

buttonhole stitch

lazy daisy stitch

The flowers are worked in white or pink buttonhole stitch and the leaves in green lazy daisy stitch.

Pigface

Pigface (also called lampranthus or mesembryanthemum) is a spreading perennial succulent with erect stems which become prostrate, with narrow cylindrical grey-green leaves. The flowers are daisy-like, in colours of cerise or pink with yellow centres. See embroidery 10.

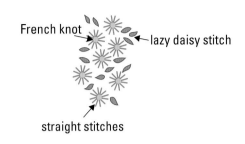

Threads

DMC 3607 (cerise)

DMC 3806 (pink)

DMC 3013 (grey-green)

The flowers are worked with a short stem stitch in cerise or pink around a central yellow French knot. The leaves are grey-green lazy daisy stitch.

Plumbago

This evergreen spreading shrub produces masses of sky blue flowerheads throughout summer. The leaves are oval in shape. See embroideries 2 and 5.

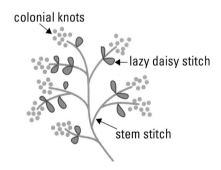

Threads

DMC 3325 (sky blue)

DMC 3348 (mid green)

The leaves are worked in mid-green lazy daisy stitch. Woody stems are worked in stem stitch in the same shade. The flowers are worked in clusters of colonial knots with two wraps in sky blue.

Poinsettia

The poinsettia originates from Mexico and flowers through winter into early summer. It has large dark green leaves and large, conspicuous bracts of bright red, pink or creamy white. The flowers are small and inconspicuous and occur in a cluster at the centre of the bracts. See embroideries 3, 10, 12, 21, and 23.

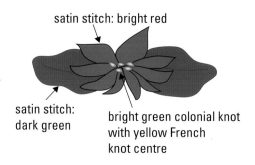

satin stitch: bright red

satin stitch: dark green

bright green colonial knot with yellow French knot centre

Threads

DMC 321 (bright red)
DMC 3346 (dark green)
DMC 3363 (bright green)
DMC 743 (yellow)

The leaves are worked in dark green satin stitch, the bracts in bright red satin stitch and the flowers in bright green colonial knots with three wraps, with a yellow French knot of one wrap in the centre.

Primrose

This attractive perennial comes in a wide range of colours, although the most commonly seen and most favoured colour is yellow. It has a fragrant perfume. See embroidery 9.

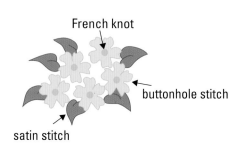

French knot

buttonhole stitch

satin stitch

Threads

DMC 3348 (mid green)
DMC 726 (soft yellow)
DMC 742 (deep yellow)

The flower is comprised of five petals worked in buttonhole stitch in soft yellow with a deep yellow centre in a five-wrap French knot. Leaves are long and worked in mid-green satin stitch at the base of the flower.

Protea

A native of South Africa, this evergreen shrub has narrow silvery grey-green leaves. The attractive flowerheads are about 13 centimetres (5 or 6 inches) long, depending on the variety, and comprise individual pink bracts. See embroidery 13.

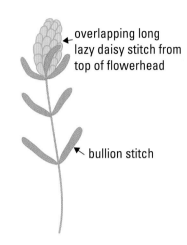

overlapping long lazy daisy stitch from top of flowerhead

bullion stitch

Threads

DMC 224 (light pink)

DMC 223 (mid pink)

DMC 3052 (green-grey)

The flowerheads are worked with two threads (one each of the light and mid pinks) in overlapping lazy daisy stitch, commencing from the tip of the flower and working to the base. Stems are done in stem stitch in two threads of green-grey. The leaves are ten-wrap bullion stitches, using two threads of green-grey.

Red-hot poker

This stately evergreen grows in clumps, with upright long-stemmed flowerheads arising from tufts of narrow light green leaves. The spikes of reddish salmon flowers are held on stout stems. See embroidery 13.

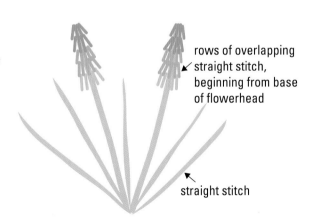

rows of overlapping straight stitch, beginning from base of flowerhead

straight stitch

Threads

DMC 472 (light green)

DMC 740 (bright orange)

DMC 741 (mid orange)

DMC 726 (mid yellow)

The long leaves are worked in two strands of light green in straight stitch. You may need couching (a small loop) to hold the stitches in place. The flowers are done in two strands of small straight stitches, working from light to dark from the base of the flower using mid yellow, mid orange and bright orange.

Rhododendron

A glorious evergreen shrub with long green leaves, blooming in early spring with large trusses of colourful flowers. See embroidery 13.

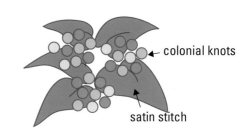

Threads

DMC 3350 *(dark pink)*

DMC 3689 *(mid pink)*

DMC 818 *(light pink)*

DMC 3363 *(bright green)*

The flowers are worked in groups of colonial knots of three wraps in any one of the pinks listed or the colour of your choice. The long leaves are worked in bright green satin stitch.

Rondeletia

This is evergreen shrub has dark green oval leaves with a brown underside. It produces dense clusters of tubular pink flowers. See embroidery 4.

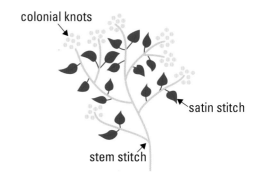

Threads

DMC 3346 *(dark green)*

DMC 962 *(mid pink)*

DMC 3045 *(light brown)*

The flowers are worked in clusters of colonial knots in a mid-pink shade and the leaves in dark green satin stitch. The stems are light brown stem stitch.

Roses

One of the most popular flowers around the world, the rose comes in an incredible variety of colours. See embroideries 2, 3, 4, 5, 8, 9, 21, 22, 23, 27, 30, 31 and 32.

rows of bullion stitch

satin stitch

stem stitch

Threads
White
DMC 321 (red)
DMC 309 (soft red)
DMC 899 (pink)
DMC 818 (pale pink)
DMC 745 (pale yellow)
DMC 744 (yellow)
DMC 3363 (mid green)
DMC 3362 (dark green)

I work the rose from the centre, starting with a light shade and making two bullion stitches of eight wraps each, changing to the darker shade and using bullion stitches of ten wraps for the outer petals. The leaves are worked with satin stitch in mid green, and the stem is a darker green stem stitch.

Snowdrops

These spring-flowering bulbs have narrow strap-shaped leaves. Each stem bears a nodding white flower with six green-tipped petals. See embroidery 13.

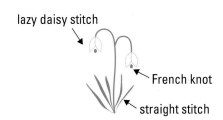

lazy daisy stitch

French knot

straight stitch

Threads
White
DMC 3348 (sap green)

The leaves are worked in stem stitch in sap green and the flowers in two French knots, each of two wraps in white, with a green one-wrap French knot between the tips of the petals.

Strelitzia

This perennial, known commonly tas the bird of paradise flower, forms a large clump of evergreen long-stalked green leaves. It has spectacular orange and blue boat-shaped flowers set into red-edged bracts. See embroideries 4, 12 and 13.

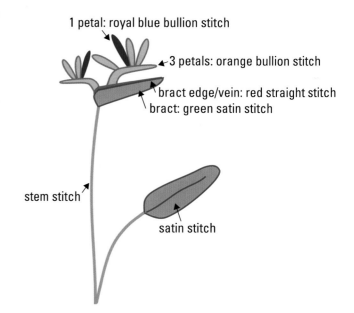

1 petal: royal blue bullion stitch

3 petals: orange bullion stitch

bract edge/vein: red straight stitch
bract: green satin stitch

stem stitch

satin stitch

Threads

DMC 971 *(orange)*

DMC 797 *(royal blue)*

DMC 915 *(red)*

DMC 3051 *(green)*

The stalks and leaves are both worked in green, the stalks in stem stitch and the leaves in satin stitch. The body of the bract is worked in satin stitch in green. The vein of the leaf and edge of the bract are in red straight stitches. Flowers are worked in bullion knots of six wraps, three petals in orange with one petal in royal blue.

Sunflower

This beautiful showy flower has a very large flowerhead with double daisy-like deep yellow petals and a large brown centre. The plant has large, serrated, oval mid-green leaves. See embroidery 13.

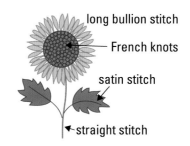

long bullion stitch

French knots

satin stitch

straight stitch

Threads

DMC 742 *(deep yellow)*

DMC 746 *(straw)*

DMC 833 *(brown)*

DMC 472 *(sap green)*

The flower petals are worked with long bullion stitches with eight wraps in deep yellow, with the centre worked in three-wrap French knots in a mixture of straw and brown. The leaves are in satin stitch, the stalks in straight stitch with couching, both worked in two threads in sap green.

Tulips

These spring-flowering bulbs are grown for their impressive upward-facing waxy flowers of many colours. The stems and long narrow leaves are grey-green. See embroidery 13.

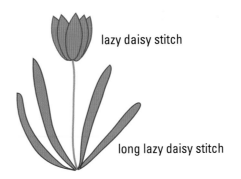

lazy daisy stitch

long lazy daisy stitch

Threads
DMC 603 (bright pink)
DMC321 (red)
DMC 444 (yellow)
DMC 971 (orange)
DMC 3052 (grey-green)

The flowers, which open wide to the sun as they age, are worked in lazy daisy stitch in bright colours of your choice. I have done the leaves in lazy daisy stitch in grey-green.

Violets

These lovely, flat-faced, rich blue-purple flowers are grown for both their colour and their perfume. The deep green leaves are flat and kidney-shaped. See embroideries 13 and 31.

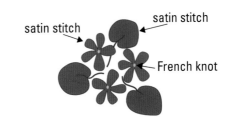

satin stitch

satin stitch

French knot

Threads
DMC 3746 (deep violet)
DMC 3347 (deep green)
DMC 972 (bright yellow)

The leaves are worked in deep green satin stitch. The flowers are worked in deep violet satin stitch, with a small yellow French knot of one wrap in the centre.

Wisteria

This vigorous woody-stemmed twining climber was popular in a past age, being grown over fences and trellises for its spectacular flowers. The highly scented mauve to pale lilac flowers fall in long trailing bunches. See embroideries 2, 18, 20, 21, 25, 27 and 28.

Threads

DMC 210 *(pale lavender)*

DMC 208 *(dark lavender)*

DMC 613 *(beige)*

DMC 3348 *(sap green)*

DMC 3045 *(light brown)*

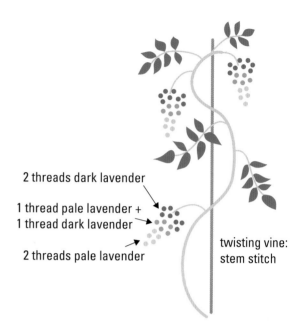

2 threads dark lavender

1 thread pale lavender +
1 thread dark lavender

2 threads pale lavender

twisting vine:
stem stitch

Starting from the top of the flowerhead, with two strands of pale lavender, work five French knots with three wraps. Change to one thread each of dark and pale lavender and work five more French knots with three wraps. Now change to two strands of dark lavender and work three to five French knots, each of three wraps, repeating until the flowerhead is the length required. This plant has lovely sap-green oval leaves on beige stems, five to seven tiny leaves per stem. They are worked in sap-green lazy daisy stitches and the twisting vine is worked in beige stem stitch. The support for the wisteria vine in embroidery 18 is worked with light brown stem stitch.

Appendix 2

This section contains embroidery instructions for all the trees depicted in the gardens included in this book. I have listed the exact thread colours used for each tree as I have embroidered them, but suggest that you match your threads with flowers, leaves, branches and tree trunks as you see fit. Single threads are used unless stated otherwise.

Unless indicated otherwise, work the stems first, then the leaves, then the flowers. See page XX for tips and requirements.

Banana

This native of the Old World tropics is not a tree but a herb bearing yellow fruit. It is composed of porous enveloping leaf sheaths terminating in large spreading leaves which often split at intervals along the prominent parallel veins. The single flowering stem bears small cream flowers with conspicuous purple bracts which grow up through the centre of the sheaths. See embroidery 20.

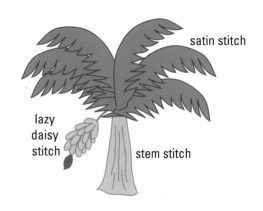

Threads

Anchor 1218 (variegated light brown)
DMC 907 (yellow-green)
DMC 307 (yellow)
DMC 3803 (purplish red)

The stem of leaf sheaths is worked in stem stitch in variegated light brown, and the leaves in yellow-green satin stitch. The fruit is worked in yellow lazy daisy stitch and the bract in three purplish red lazy daisy stitches at the tip (bottom) of the bunch of fruit.

Bookleaf pine

This is a short decorative pine used commonly at entrances and in formal gardens. See embroidery 10.

Threads

DMC 3364 *(light green)*
DMC 3363 *(mid green)*
DMC 3362 *(dark green)*

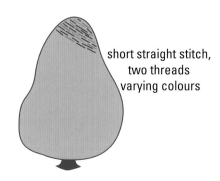

short straight stitch, two threads varying colours

Using two threads, one each of two of the above greens to mix the shades, work in small slanting straight stitches in varying directions, starting at the top of the tree and working towards the base, mixing the shades as you rethread the needle.

Bottle tree

This tree of south-east Queensland, related to the kurrajong, has a bottle-shaped trunk with rough-textured dark grey bark and deep green elongated leaves. See embroidery 18.

Threads

DMC 3347 *(dark green)*
DMC 535 *(dark grey)*

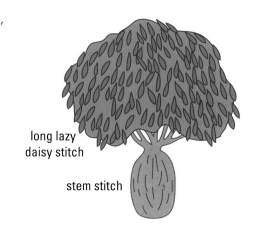

long lazy daisy stitch

stem stitch

The branches and trunk are worked with dark grey in close stem stitch and the leaves in long dark green lazy daisy stitches.

Bunya pine

This majestic Queensland tree presents something of a challenge to the embroiderer. It is shown in embroideries 22 and 32.

Threads

YLI 947 brown stranded silk
DMC 898 (dark brown)
DMC 3362 (deep green)

Work the trunk first, padding it with long and short vertical straight stitches in six strands of dark brown. Then, using one thread of brown stranded silk, stitch around the trunk from bottom to the top. If you cannot buy the right colour, dye a beige-coloured thread in patches to produce a variegated effect, using tea bags or a brown Pentel FabricFun pastel dye stick, which is easy to use. Set the dye with a warm iron. I did the branches next with a long deep green straight stitch, caught in the middle with a loop stitch to hold the shape, with deep green leaf stems in straight stitch coming from each branch. The leaves are very spiky and sharp—to convey this effect use small straight stitches in deep green.

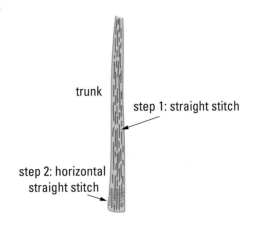

trunk

step 1: straight stitch

step 2: horizontal straight stitch

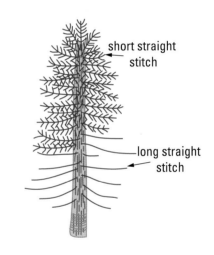

short straight stitch

long straight stitch

Cassia

This is a beautiful tree about three to four metres in height. It flowers in summer with long drooping clusters of bright yellow flowers. See embroidery 30.

Threads

DMC 307 *(yellow)*

DMC 3362 *(dark green)*

DMC 840 *(dark brown)*

DMC 3371 *(brownish black)*

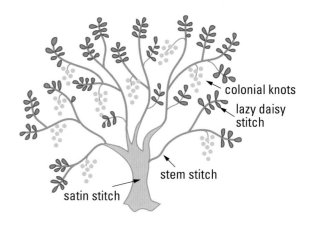

The flowers are worked in three-wrap yellow colonial knots, starting at the tip of the cluster. The leaves are five to a stem and worked in dark green lazy daisy stitch. The small branches and stems are dark brown stem stitch. After flowering the cylindrical seedpods appear, about 30 cm (12 inches) in length and dark brownish black in colour. The trunk is worked in dark brown satin stitch. If you wish to show the seedpods, work them from the bottom to the top in brownish black satin stitch, working around the bean.

Cumquat

This Asiatic citrus tree is often used as an interesting feature plant in large pots as in embroidery 29. It bears small oval to round orange fruit which makes a delicious tangy jam.

Threads

DMC 741 *(orange)*

DMC 611 *(light brown)*

DMC 905 *(bright green)*

DMC 356 *(terra cotta)*

DMC 524 *(grey-green)*

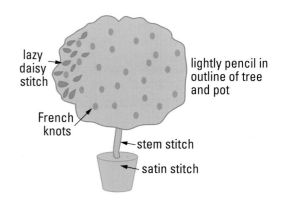

The trunk and branches are worked in grey-green stem stitch. The bright green glossy leaves which are worked in lazy daisy stitch. The fruit is worked in bright orange French knots with two twists. The terracotta pot is worked in satin stitch.

Cypress pine

Cypress pines are fast-growing pyramidal trees, best fashioned with three different coloured threads. A golden cypress is depicted in embroidery 31 and other cypresses appear in embroideries 3, 4, 8, 21, 22 and 29.

Threads

DMC 3822 (yellow)
DMC 472 (soft green)
DMC 895 (yellow-green)
DMC 3362 (dark green)
DMC 3363 (mid green)
DMC 3364 (light green)
DMC 645 (mid grey)

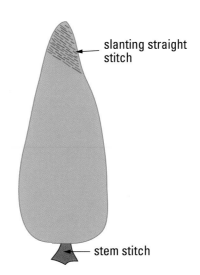

slanting straight stitch

stem stitch

The golden cypress is embroidered in short slanting straight stitches in varying directions with two strands of thread. Use one strand of yellow and alternate one thread of soft green and yellow-green in the needle.

A green cypress is embroidered in the same manner, using a mixture of two threads of either dark green, mid green or light green to produce the effect required.

The trunk is worked in mid-grey stem stitch, working from the base to the line of the foliage.

Eucalyptus

There are over 200 species of
Australian eucalypts or gum trees.
One of my favourites is Eucalyptus
cladocalyx, the Sugar Gum, which
has a straight trunk with smooth
pale bark and grows to at least 10
metres. See embroideries 6, 12, 16,
18, 19, 20, 21, 22, 27, 30 and 31.
The trunks of a rainforest species
appear in embroidery 16, with the
foliage framing the building that
of various unidentified subtropical
rainforest species.

Threads

DMC 61 (light variegated brown)
DMC 907 (bright green)
DMC 3346 (medium green)
DMC 3045 (light brown)
DMC 3052 (grey-green)
DMC 3051 (dark green)
DMC 370 (mid brown)
DMC 3012 (brown-green)

top half of crescent of foliage:
work from right to left in
buttonhole stitch

lower half of crescent:
turn work upside down and
work from right to left in
buttonhole stitch

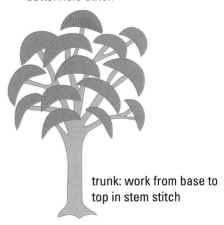

trunk: work from base to
top in stem stitch

The 'crescents' of foliage are embroidered in buttonhole stitch, using light grey-
green on top and brown-green on the bottom half. I turn the work upside down to
embroider the bottom part of the foliage. The stems bearing this foliage should
match the trunk in colour and be worked in stem stitch. The trunk is worked in
light brown or mid-brown stem stitch, starting at the base. The trunks of the large
gums in embroidery 16 are worked in light variegated brown stem stitch, and the
rainforest foliage is worked in a mixture of green threads in lazy daisy stitch.

Flowering gum

This very beautiful flowering tree blooms in winter and spring and attracts many species of parrots. The flowers may be pink, red, white or apricot with a boss of stamens in large clusters. See embroideries 12 and 14.

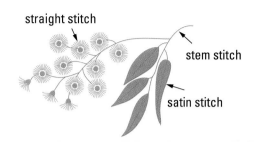

Threads

DMC 3326 *(pink)*

DMC 3348 *(soft green)*

DMC 420 *(brown)*

The flowers comprise many stamens done with straight stitches in pink or another shade around a central point. The circular centres are a straight stitch couched into shape in the same soft green colour as the leaves. The long thin leaves are worked in satin stitch. The stem-stitched stems and the satin-stitched pods of the flowers are worked in brown.

Frangipani

This deciduous tree from tropical Mexico bears clusters of flowers in white, cream, pink or apricot with a beautiful perfume. It is shown in embroideries 7, 12, 20, 21, 23 and 25.

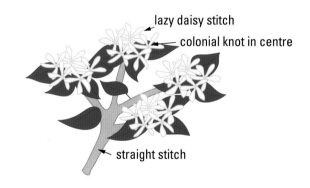

Threads

White

DMC 3078 *(cream)*

DMC 973 *(soft yellow)*

DMC 370 *(mid brown)*

DMC 3347 *(mid green)*

The five white or coloured petals of the flowers are worked in lazy daisy stitch with the flush of soft yellow at the base of the petals worked in a colonial knot. The stem is filled in with mid-brown straight stitches and the leaves, which can be up to 30 cm (12 inches) long, are worked in mid-green satin stitch.

Grass tree

These ancient and unusual plants may have short or tall trunks. They have a crown of long narrow grass-like leaves and often a skirt of older dead leaves. The small creamy white flowers are crowded along a thick flower spike. See embroidery 15.

Threads

Black
DMC 3046 (cream-brown)
DMC 3790 (mid brown)
DMC 3347 (mid green)

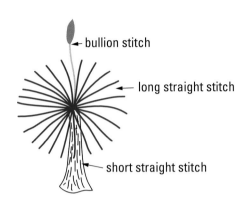

Leaves are worked in straight stitches in mid green. The flower stem is worked in straight stitch with two threads in cream-brown, while the flower head is worked in ten-wrap bullion stitch with two threads in mid brown. The stem of the tree is worked with short straight stitches in black.

Holly

The various species of holly range in size from small shrubs to tall specimen trees. The leaves can be smooth-edged or spiny and vary considerably in colour, either variegated in a number of patterns or solid bright green. The small white flowers develop attractive red berries. See embroidery 32.

Threads

DMC 3362 (deep green)
DMC 321 (bright red)
YLI 9479 stranded silk (mid brown)

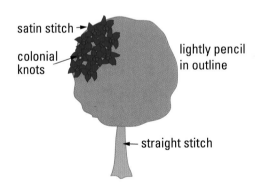

The shape of the tree is lightly outlined in pencil, then filled in with leaves and berries. The leaves are worked in bright green satin stitch, the berries in colonial knots of three twists. The trunk is worked in mid-brown stem stitch, starting at the base of the tree.

Jacaranda

What a wonderful sight it is in November and December when the jacarandas are in full bloom—though students with approaching examinations may fail to appreciate them. See embroideries 3, 9, 11, 18, 19, 20, 21, 22, 23, 25, 31 and 32.

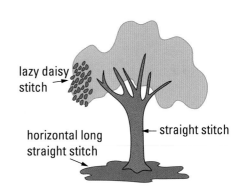

Threads

DMC 341 (light blue-purple)

DMC 340 (dark blue-purple)

DMC 844 (deep grey)

The shape of the tree is lightly outlined in pencil, then filled in with flowers. The flowers are worked in lazy daisy stitch in the two shades of blue-purple, alternating the colours. The trunk is a rugged rough texture, worked with deep grey in one thread, using slanting and vertical straight stitches to produce the rough effect. The carpet of purple under the tree is worked in long straight stitches of different lengths.

Lagerstroemia

This lovely tree is commonly called pride of India or crepe myrtle. It produces dense trusses of purple, pink or white flowers in late summer. See embroidery 12.

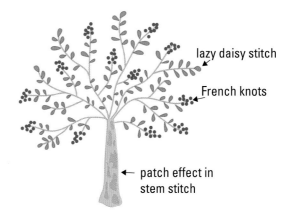

Threads

DMC 3716 (pink)

DMC 3348 (yellow-green)

DMC 422 (cream-brown)

DMC 3828 (gold-brown)

The flowers are worked first in long heads of eight French knots of three twists. The branches are long and slender and change colour as they shed their bark. Work branches and trunks in two-thread stem stitch using cream-brown and gold-brown combined to achieve the mottled effect. The leaves are worked in lazy daisy stitch in a yellow-green shade.

Lemon tree

Every farm had one or more lemon tree. See embroidery 21.

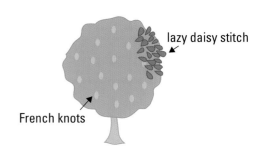

Threads

DMC 907 *(bright green)*

DMC 3829 *(mid brown)*

DMC 444 *(mid yellow)*

The trunk is worked in mid-brown stem stitch, the leaves in bright green lazy daisy and the fruit in mid-yellow French knots with five wraps.

Leopard tree

This is a tall gracious deciduous tree with very fine leaves and a smooth elegant soft grey trunk which becomes beautifully multi-coloured when shedding its bark. See embroidery 24.

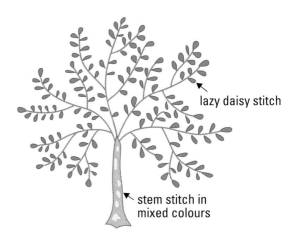

Threads

Anchor 1218 *(variegated light brown)*

DMC 53 *(variegated light grey)*

DMC 3078 *(clotted cream)*

DMC 469 *(fern green)*

The leaves are worked in fern-green lazy daisy stitch. The mottled trunk should be worked in stem stitch in a mixture of variegated grey and light brown, and clotted cream.

Magnolia

Another of my favourite trees, this is a native of eastern North America. There are evergreen and deciduous types but all have wonderful, very fragrant large creamy white or pink flowers with five petals. See embroideries 27 and 31.

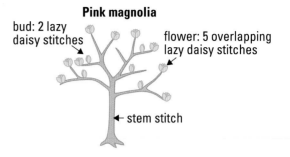

Pink magnolia

bud: 2 lazy daisy stitches

flower: 5 overlapping lazy daisy stitches

stem stitch

Threads

White
DMC 3078 (cream)
DMC 3688 (dark pink)
DMC 3363 (dark green)
DMC 840 (beige-brown)

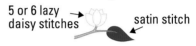

Cream magnolia

5 or 6 lazy daisy stitches

satin stitch

The flowers are worked in cream or pink lazy daisy stitch using two threads. The large glossy leaves are worked in dark green satin stitch. The stout branches have smooth beige-brown bark worked in stem stitch. The pink magnolia loses its leaves before flowering.

Mango

This tropical evergreen tree has slim, glossy, leathery leaves. The flower is cream in colour with a central stem bearing spikes of flowers all around. The fruit is a smooth irregular oval in shape, green ripening to a beautiful gold and hanging from the branches. See embroidery 12.

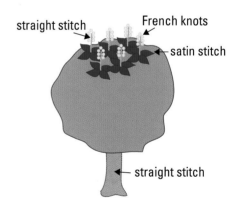

straight stitch

French knots

satin stitch

straight stitch

Threads

DMC 3363 (deep green)
DMC 3078 (cream)
DMC 645 (mid grey)

The leaves are worked in deep green satin stitch. The trunk is embroidered in mid-grey stem stitch, starting at the ground and working upwards, and the flower spike is worked in stem stitch in the same shade. The flowers are worked in cream French knots on either side of the flower stems.

Norfolk Island pine

This handsome pine is widely planted along Australian coastal areas and is important for its timber. It is only suitable for larger gardens because of its size. Young potted specimens make excellent Christmas trees. See embroideries 8, 19 and 21.

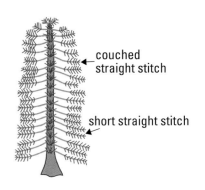

Threads

DMC 3799 (dark grey)

DMC 3346 (dark green)

The trunk is worked in dark grey stem stitch, starting from the base of the tree. Branches are also dark grey, using straight stitches caught in position in the middle with a loop stitch. The leaves are short straight stitches of dark green.stem stitch, working from base upwards

Palms

Several species of palm are widely used as landscape features. They mostly have long graceful feather-like fronds produced continuously from the centre of the top of the trunk. The flowers are produced at the top of the trunk and usually burst forth with cream flowers. Palms appear in embroideries 2, 11, 18, 23 and 31.

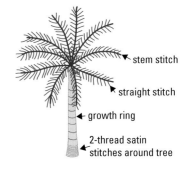

Threads

DMC 3052 (mid green)

DMC 3347 (dark green)

DMC 3051 (very dark green)

DMC 3022 (milk brown)

DMC 647 (grey)

DMC 3012 (brown-green)

young palms have no stem

The trunk is embroidered in two-thread satin stitch, worked across, not vertically, in colours varying from milk brown to a grey shade. Each year's growth is marked by a dark brown-green ring, also in satin stitch. (Larger trunks may be padded.) The fronds vary from mid green to a darker shade, depending on the species, and are worked in straight stitch onto the midrib, which is worked in stem stitch in the same shade.

Peach tree

The flowering peach is grown as an ornamental tree, not for its insignificant fruit. They are deciduous, dropping their leaves before coming into full flower. See embroideries 8, 26 and 28.

Threads

DMC 3716 *(mid pink)*
DMC 962 *(dark pink)*
DMC 3781 *(dark brown)*

Work the flowers in pale or bright pink in groups of colonial knots with three wraps. The trunk is worked in dark brown stem stitch, and the branches are done in dark brown straight stitches. If the branches are long, catch them in the middle with a loop stitch.

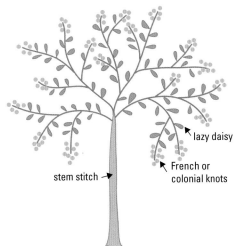

Peltophorum

These lovely hardy evergreens grow to about 10 metres and have attractive soft green foliage and long trusses of bright yellow flowers. See embroideries 6 and 7.

Threads

DMC 743 *(bright yellow)*
DMC 368 *(soft green)*
DMC 840 *(soft brown)*

Work the leaves in soft green lazy daisy stitch, the stem in soft brown stem stitch and the long fronds of flowers in bright yellow French or colonial knots.

Pencil pine

These tall elegant trees can make an eye-catching focal point in a garden design. See embroideries 3, 4, 8, 21, 22 and 29.

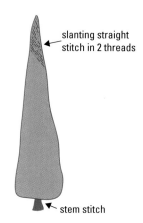

slanting straight stitch in 2 threads

stem stitch

Threads

DMC 3362 (dark green)
DMC 3363 (medium green)
DMC 3346 (very dark green)
DMC 610 (dark brown)

The foliage is worked with two-thread slanting straight stitches in varying directions using different combinations of the three greens. Work from the top, with two shades of cotton in your needle at the same time. Work the trunk in dark brown stem stitch, starting at the base and working up to the foliage.

Pink cassia

This tree is a feature in the grounds of St Paul's Anglican Cathedral in Rockhampton where it always stands out when in bloom. It has long sprays of fine leaves and a cloud of pale pink flowers which appear in the spring, completely smothering the branches. See embroidery 11.

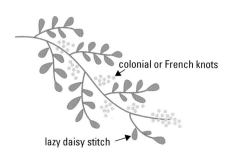

colonial or French knots

lazy daisy stitch

Threads

DMC 3716 (mid pink)
DMC 3364 (mid green)
DMC 610 (dark brown)

Lightly pencil in branch positions and smother with flowers and leaves. The flowers are worked with four-wrap colonial knots or French knots, branches in dark brown stem stitch and the mid-green leaves in lazy daisy stitch.

Poinciana

This is a deciduous native of
Madagascar with a lovely shape and a
magnificent lengthy floral summer
display in scarlet, orange or rarely
yellow. I was having trouble with the
trunk when my husband handed me a
fistful of threads from the floor. I
grabbed them and stuffed down the
trunk to create the relief effect for
which I was looking. The leaves are
compound and up to 60 cm
(24 inches) long and the flowers
develop in clusters. See embroidery 28.

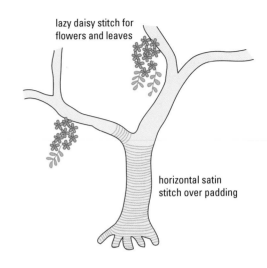

lazy daisy stitch for
flowers and leaves

horizontal satin
stitch over padding

Threads
YLI 47 (grey silk floss)
DMC 321 (red)
DMC 900 (orange-red)
DMC 581 (yellow-green)
DMC 3347 (soft green)
DMC 3348 (mid green)

Work the trunk with grey silk floss in satin stitch and then stuff it with old threads
or strips of cotton wool. Flowers in two shades of red and orange-red are worked
separately, using lazy daisy stitch, five orange blooms to three of red. The leaves on
shortish stalks form fronds and merge with the flowers towards the ends of the
branches. They are worked in short lazy daisy stitches in three shades of green.

Pussy willow

This deciduous upright multi-branched tree has yellow-green stems which turn to yellow-brown. They contrast nicely with the milk-brown catkins which appear in early spring before the foliage reappears. See embroidery 13.

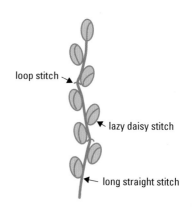

Threads

DMC 453 *(milk brown)*
DMC 869 *(mid brown)*

The stems are worked in one straight stitch of mid brown, caught in two places by a loop to represent the notches in the branch. The catkins are worked in two-thread lazy daisy stitch in milk brown.

Silky oak

This Australian native is partly deciduous. Its long fine fronds are a grey-green shade and form a brownish carpet below the tree during winter. In spring the rich gold flowers appear and the mess of winter is forgiven. See embroideries 9 and 19.

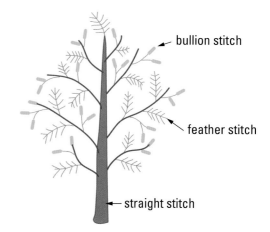

Threads

DMC 3363 *(grey-green)*
DMC 726 *(bright yellow)*
DMC 370 *(mid brown)*

The trunk is rough-textured and worked in short and long straight stitches of mid brown, working up the trunk and branches. The leaves are worked in grey-green feather stitch. The flowers are worked in bright yellow bullion stitches with six wraps.

Umbrella tree

The umbrella tree has multiple trunks emanating from the base. The foliage comprises 'rosettes' of as many as fifteen light green leaves, elliptical in shape and up to 30 cm (12 inches) in length, radiating from a single point at the end of yellowish green leaf stems. The flower stalk is black-red in colour bearing a spike of red flowers. See embroideries 20 and 21.

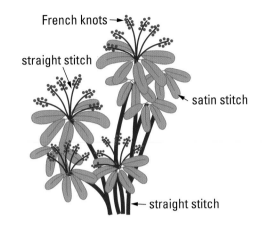

Threads

DMC 3346 *(light green)*

DMC 907 *(yellow-green)*

DMC 3803 *(black-red)*

DMC 321 *(red)*

Work leaves in light green satin stitch with smaller leaves in yellow-green satin stitch. Long fronds radiate from the top, the red flowers being done in two-wrap French knots. The flower stems are one straight stitch of black red. The trunk is worked in light green straight stitch.

Wattle

Wattle is the common name for the many acacias native to Australia; the Golden Wattle is appropriately our national flower, its colours akin to our sporting colours of green and gold. Many wattles are quick growing and they take many forms—some with dark green feathery leaves, others with simple linear leaves. *Acacia podalyrifolia*, the Silver Wattle of Queensland depicted in these embroideries, has rounded silver-green leaves along its branches. See embroideries 4, 10, 21 and 29.

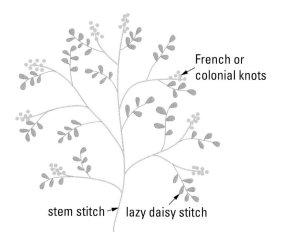

French or colonial knots

stem stitch   lazy daisy stitch

Threads
DMC 742 (bright yellow)
DMC 3013 (silver-green)

The leaves are worked in short lazy daisy stitches in silver green. The tiny flowers, usually bright yellow but sometimes an orange-yellow, grow in clusters and are embroidered in French or colonial knots with two wraps. The stem is also silver-green and done in stem stitch.

Wisteria tree

Wisteria cultivated as a standard, or tree, is uncommon. It generally grows only to about four metres, with soft flowing branches. The soft green leaves and the flower remain the same as on the wisteria vine. See embroideries 10 and 29.

Threads

DMC 208 *(dark mauve)*

DMC 211 *(light mauve)*

DMC 371 *(beige)*

DMC 3348 *(soft green)*

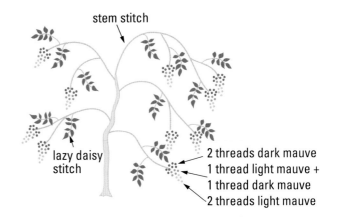

stem stitch

lazy daisy stitch

2 threads dark mauve
1 thread light mauve +
1 thread dark mauve
2 threads light mauve

The flowers are a mixture of light and dark mauves worked in French knots as follows. Start at the tip of the flowerhead with two threads of dark mauve and work four or five French knots, then change to one thread each of dark mauve and light mauve and work five knots. Then work another five knots using two threads of light mauve. The trunk and flower stems are done in beige stem stitch and the leaves in soft green lazy daisy stitch, all in a single thread.

About the author: Betty Woolcock

Betty was born at Maryborough, Queensland, into a talented family heavily involved in business and in the community. Her father was a builder who drafted his own building designs and her mother, Emilee Moller, who had trained in Sydney as a florist, later became an artist well known in south-east and central Queensland. Betty won an art teacher's scholarship but was drawn to floral art in which she established a thriving business. Among her many achievements was gaining her licence to fly a Tiger Moth. She sacrificed all this to marry Bryan, a veterinary surgeon, and so began a number of moves around Queensland, initially to Barcaldine, then Toowoomba, Rockhampton and finally Brisbane.

In Toowoomba Betty was involved as a volunteer with a mothercraft centre when she was asked to fill in temporarily as Director of the Glennie Memorial School kindergarten. Four years later she resigned with the arrival of her first child. After nine years and two children, Bryan accepted an appointment in Rockhampton. There Betty became heavily involved in an Anglican charity but also taught floral art at the local adult education centre. Seven years later the family moved to Brisbane where Betty and Bryan now enjoy their six grandchildren.

With her two children at secondary schools, Betty established a very successful florist business at Indooroopilly and in 1982 started the Queensland Academy of Floristry, which twenty years on has produced many hundreds of graduates in floral art. She received advanced experience at a Master Design School of Floristry in the United States and at the Constance Spry School of Floristry in the United Kingdom. Having sold her interest in the business and the academy, Betty turned to another craft, namely quilting. Not entirely satisfied with appliqué, she embroidered several quilts and became sold on embroidery, an art form she had enjoyed as a schoolgirl. Then followed the embroidering of the six homes she had lived in and a passion to embroider old houses and gardens, the subject of this book. Betty has been generous with her time and her desire to pass on her skills and currently has four groups of ladies who benefit from her encouragement and her talents. She is an active member of a quilter's group and is in demand as a guest speaker on these crafts.